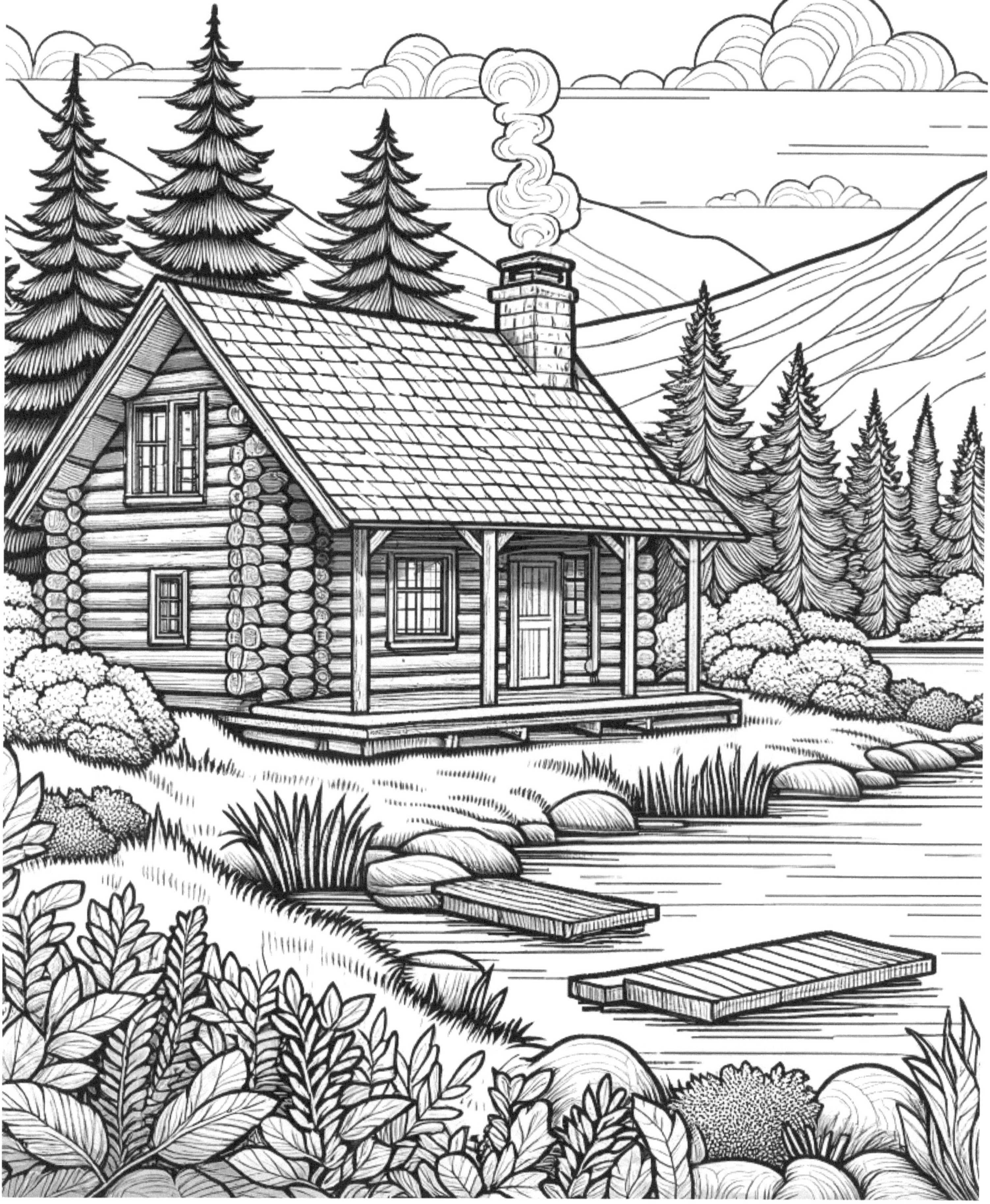

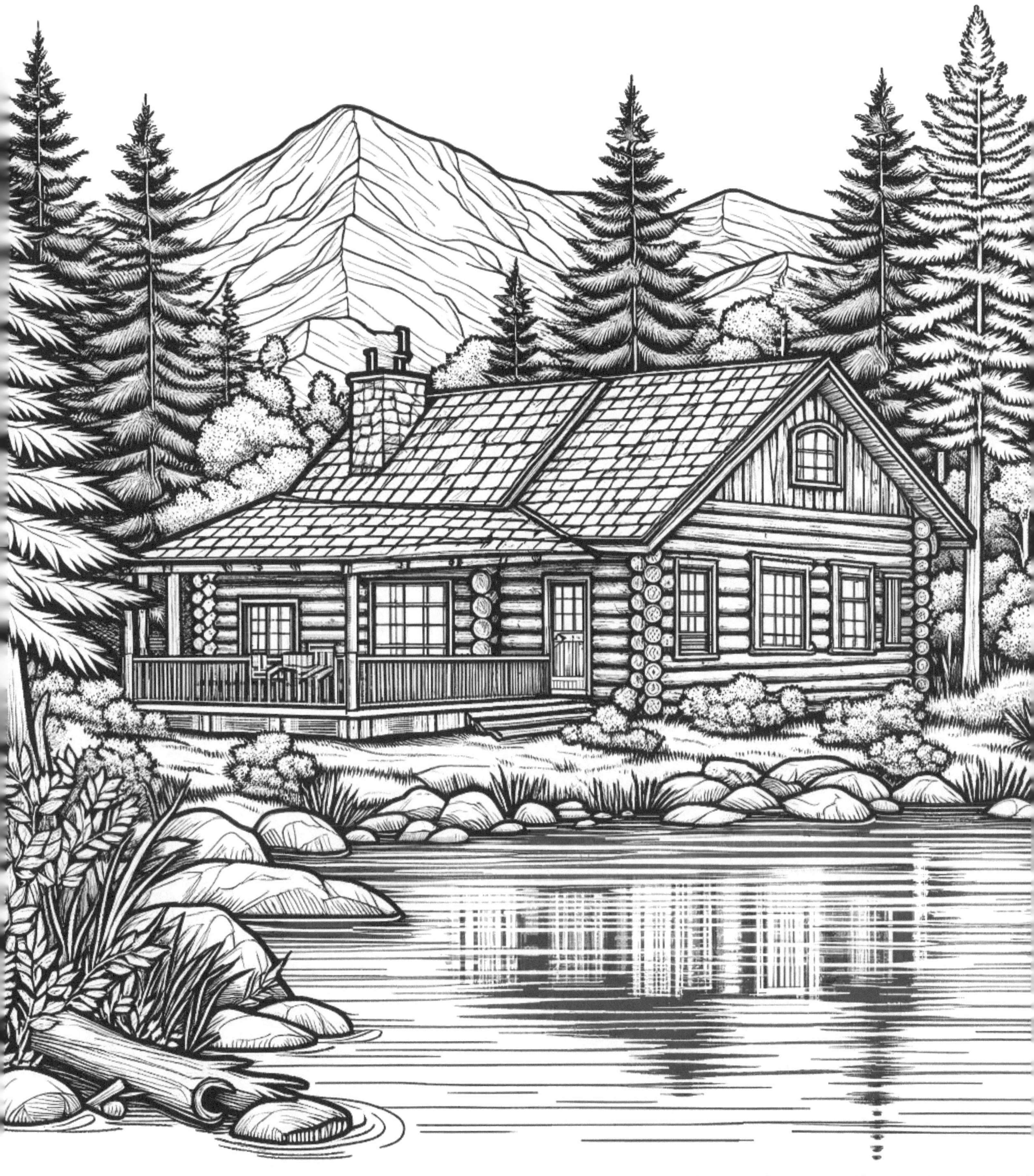

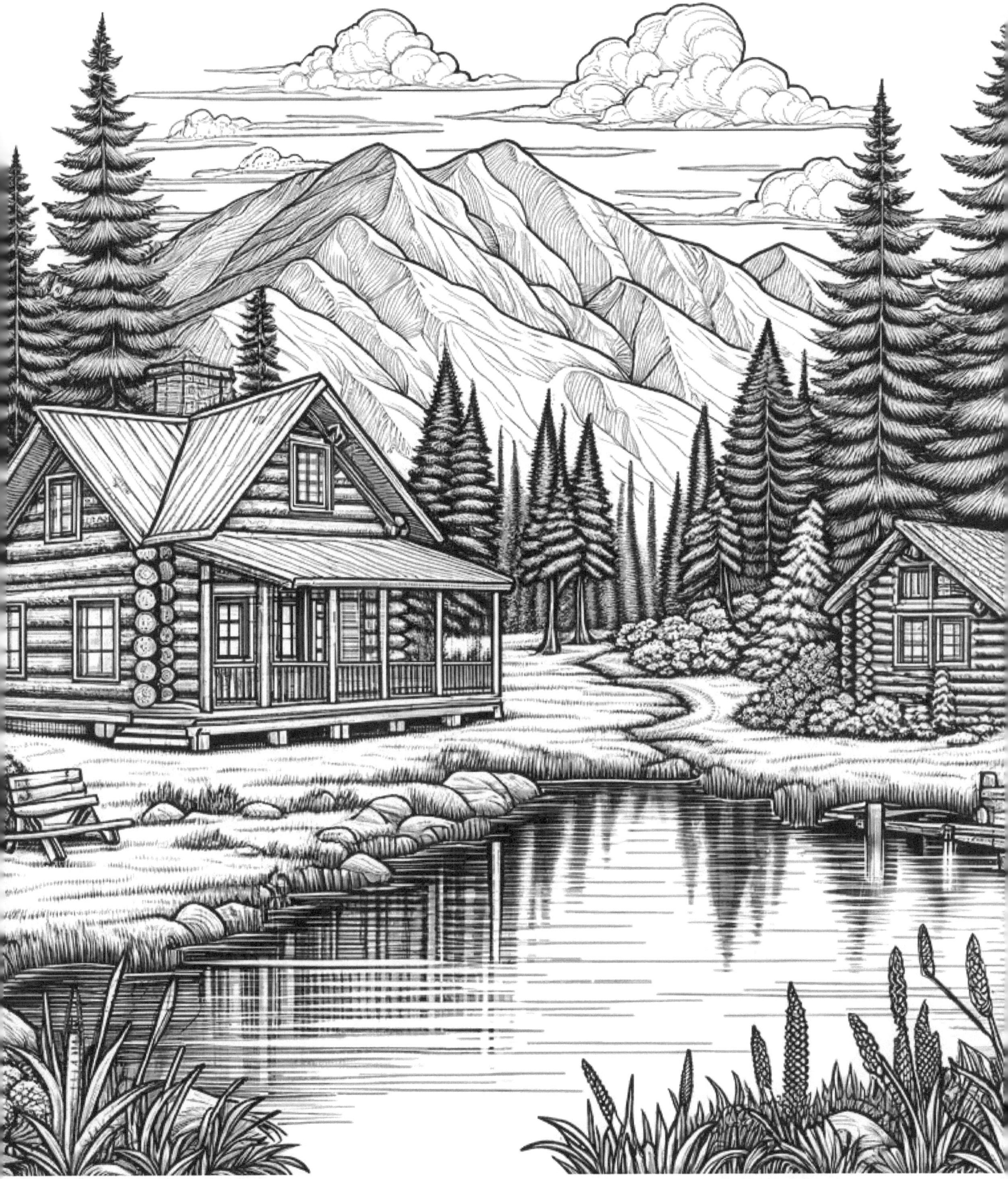

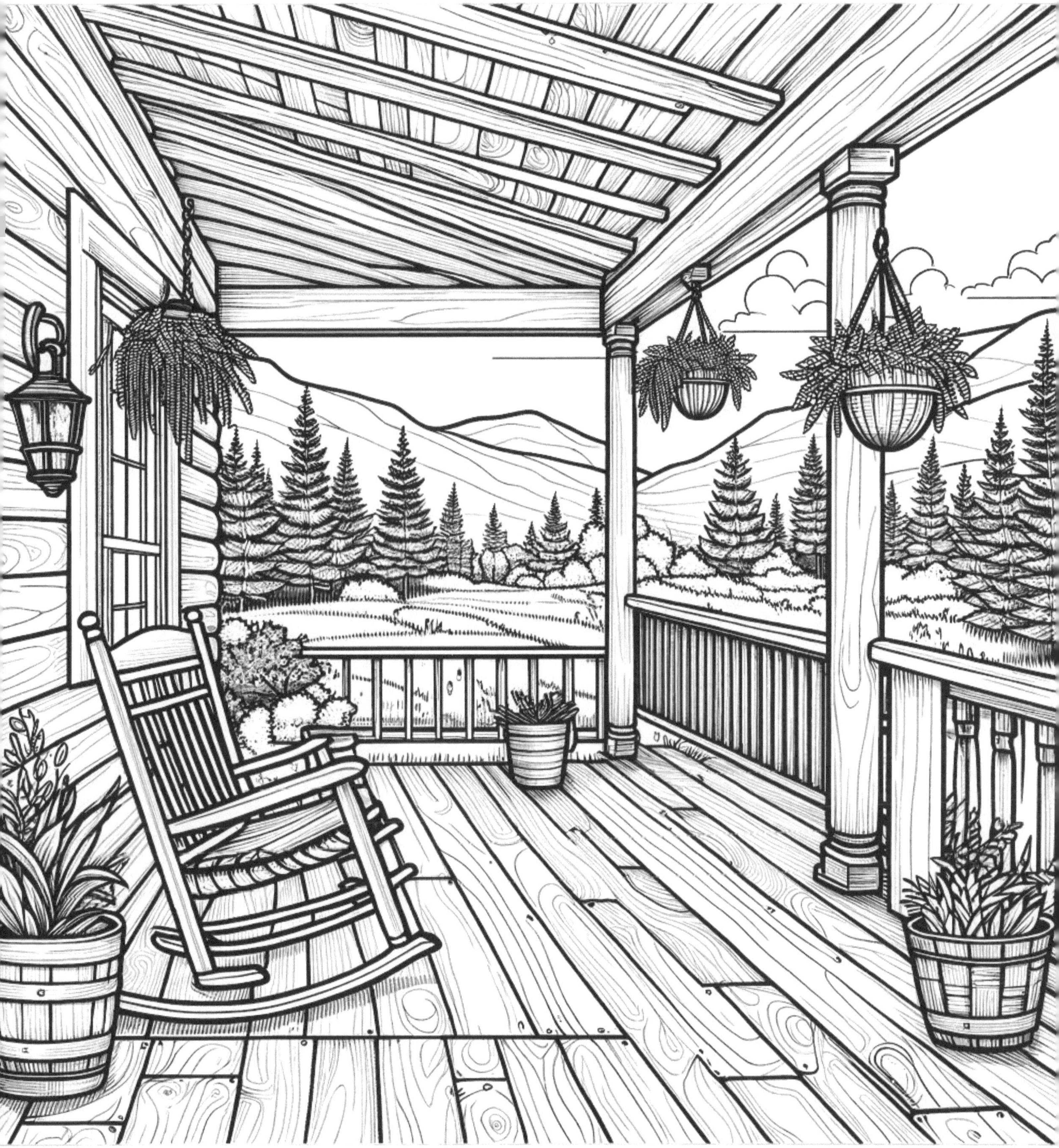

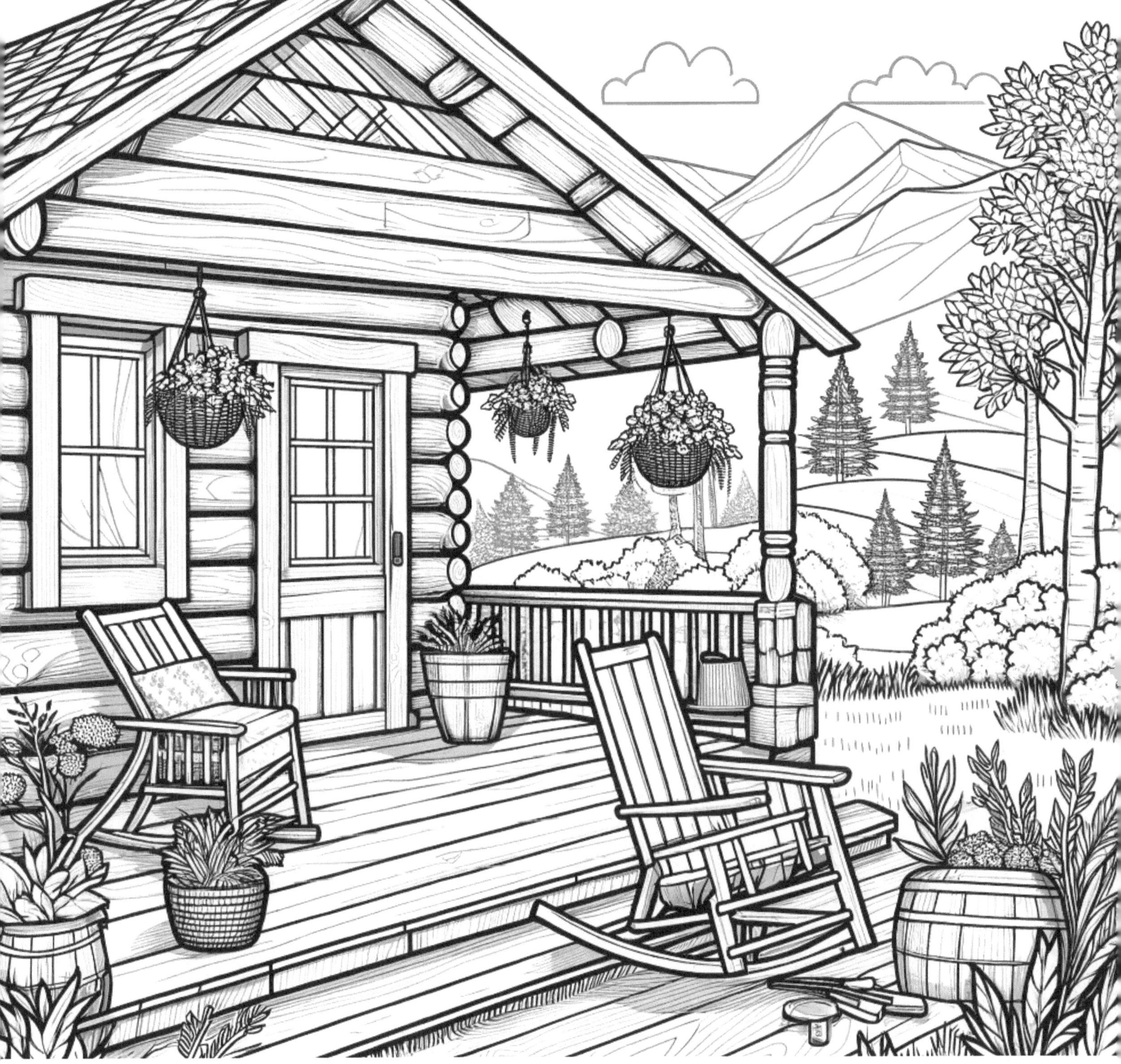

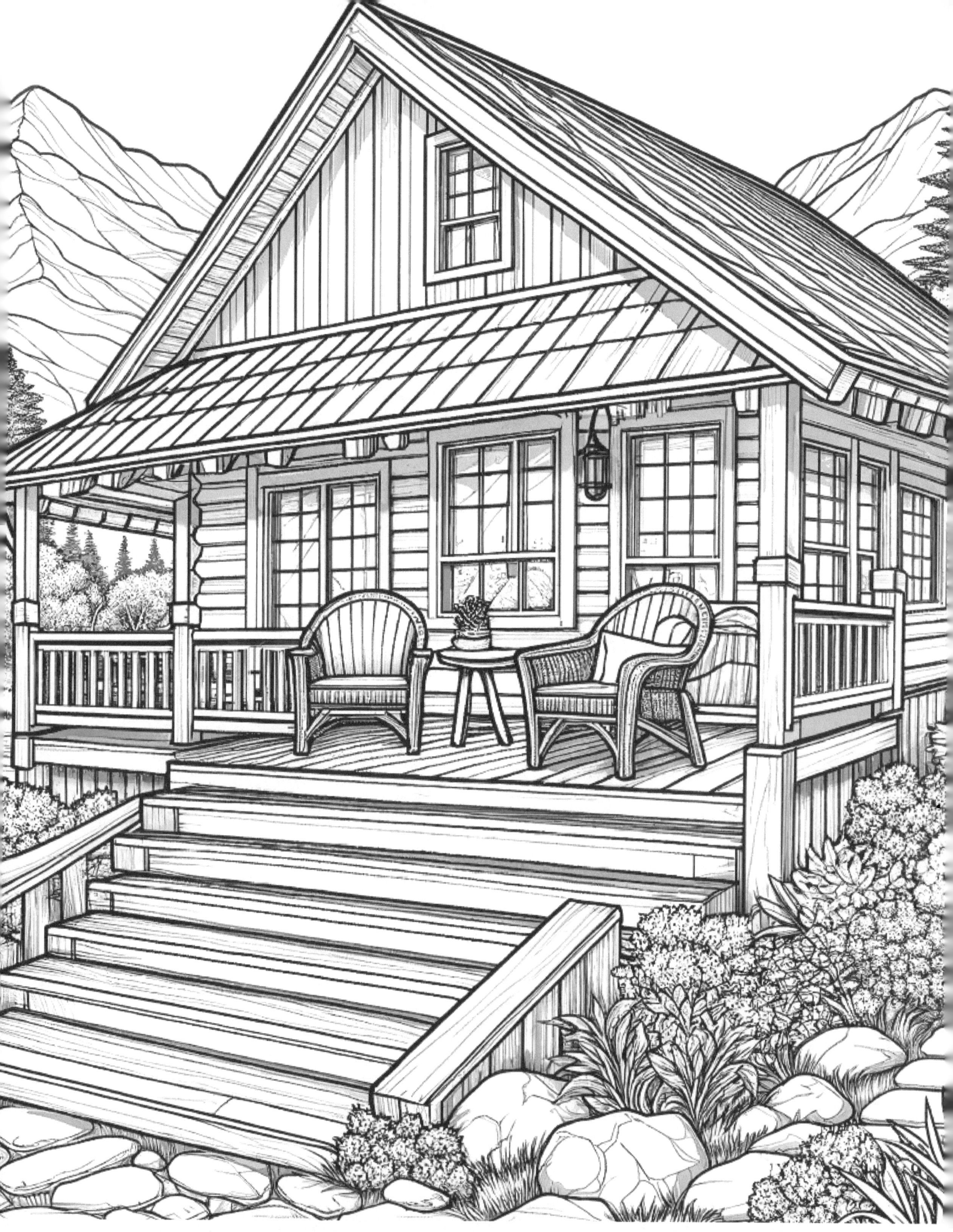

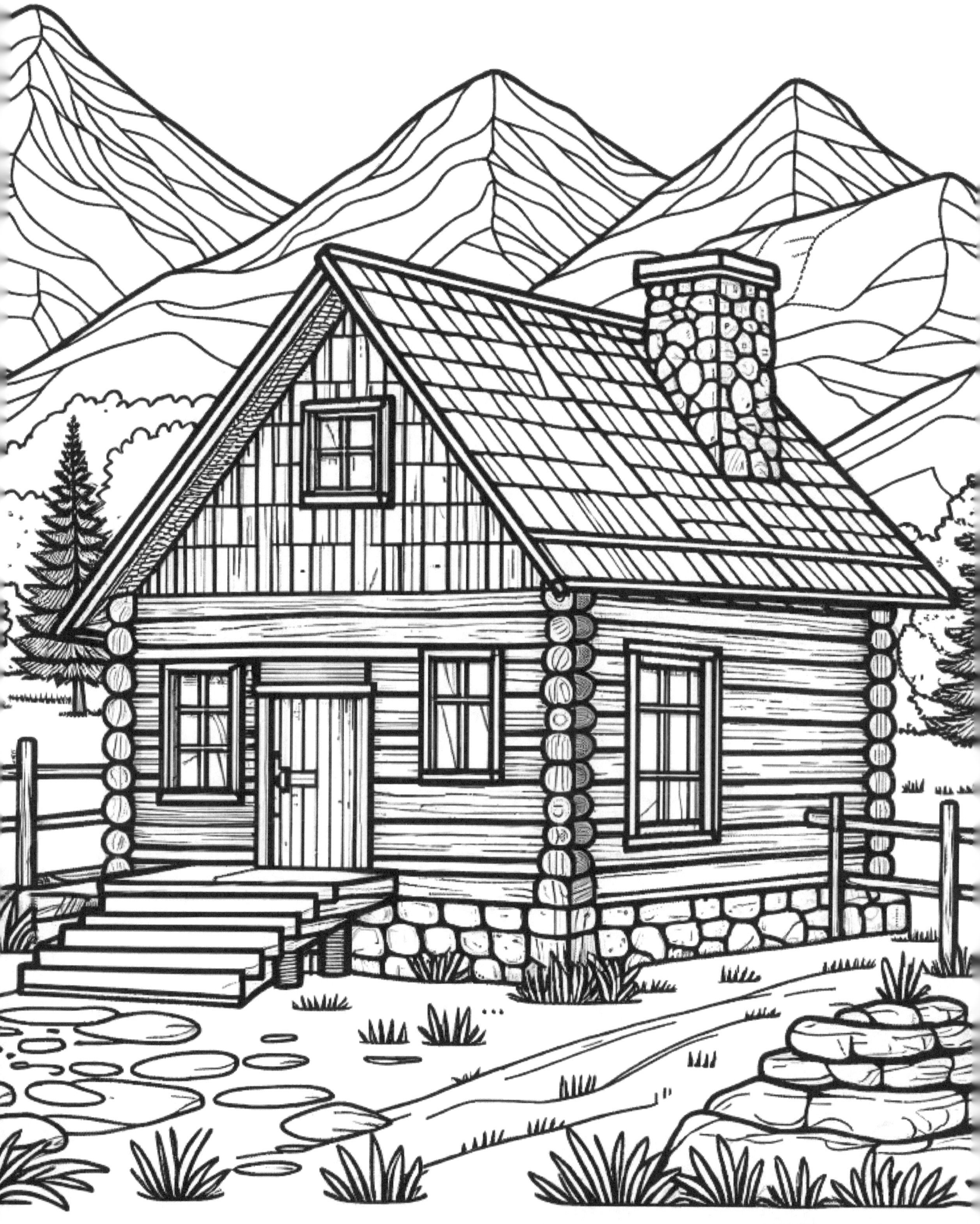

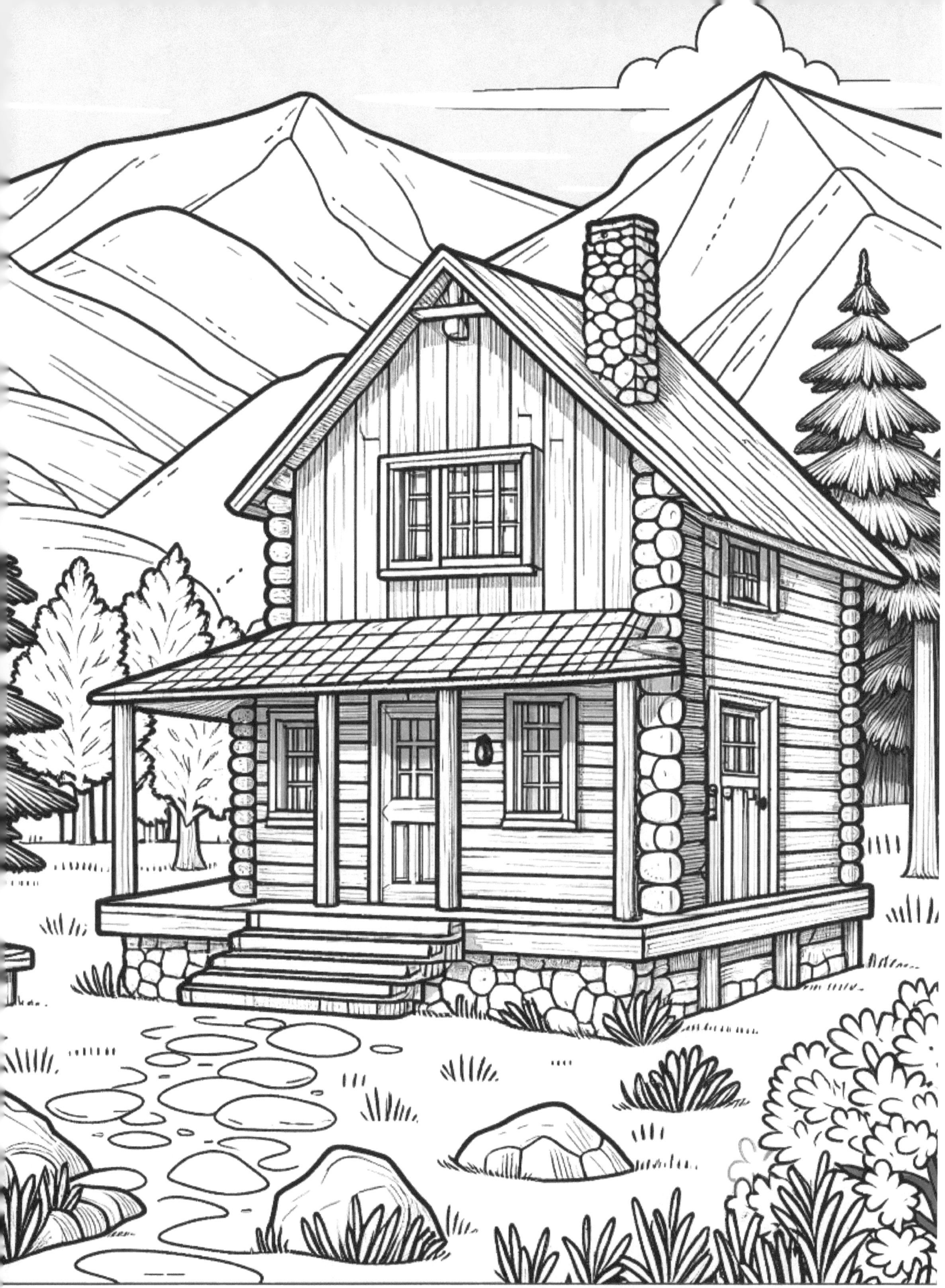

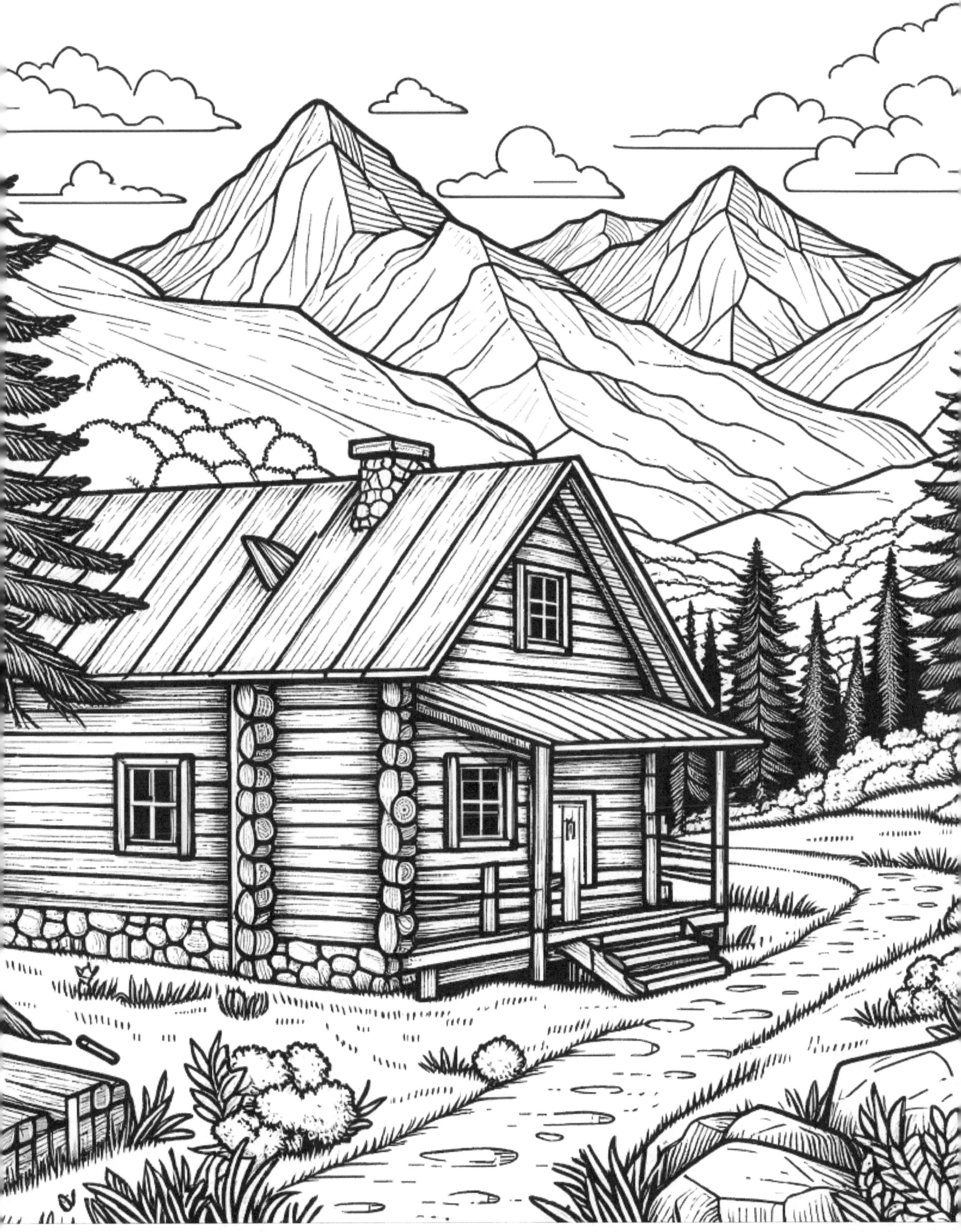

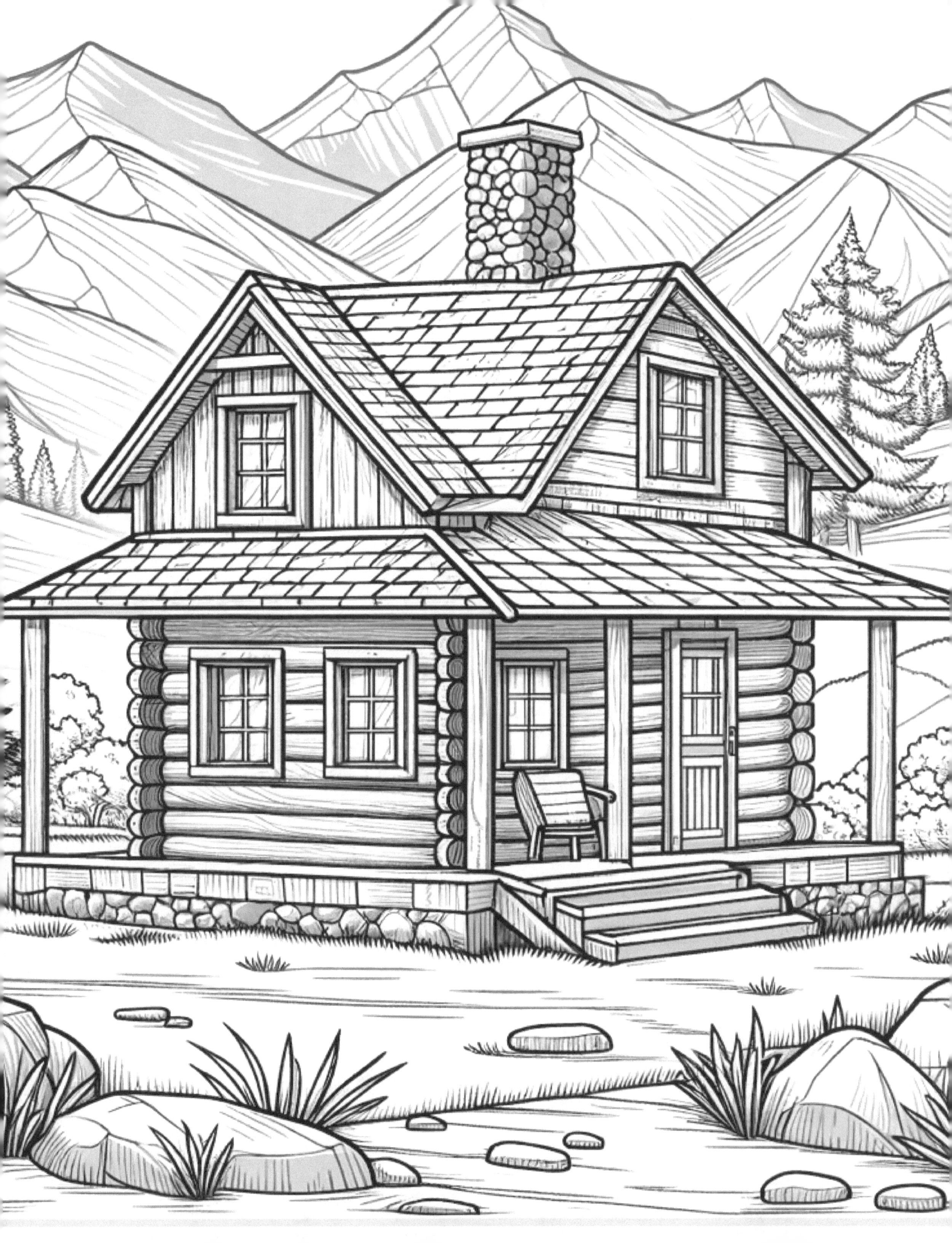

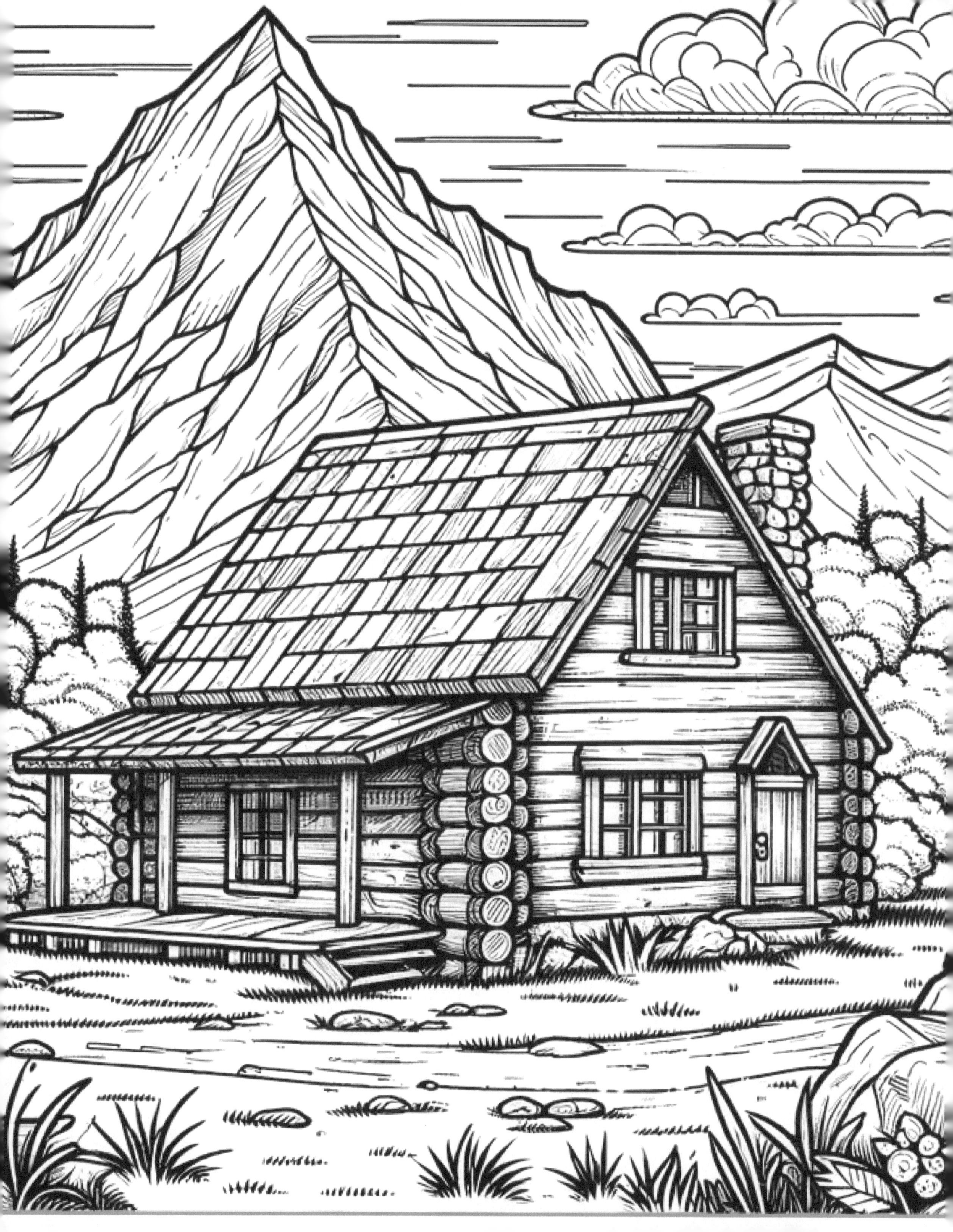

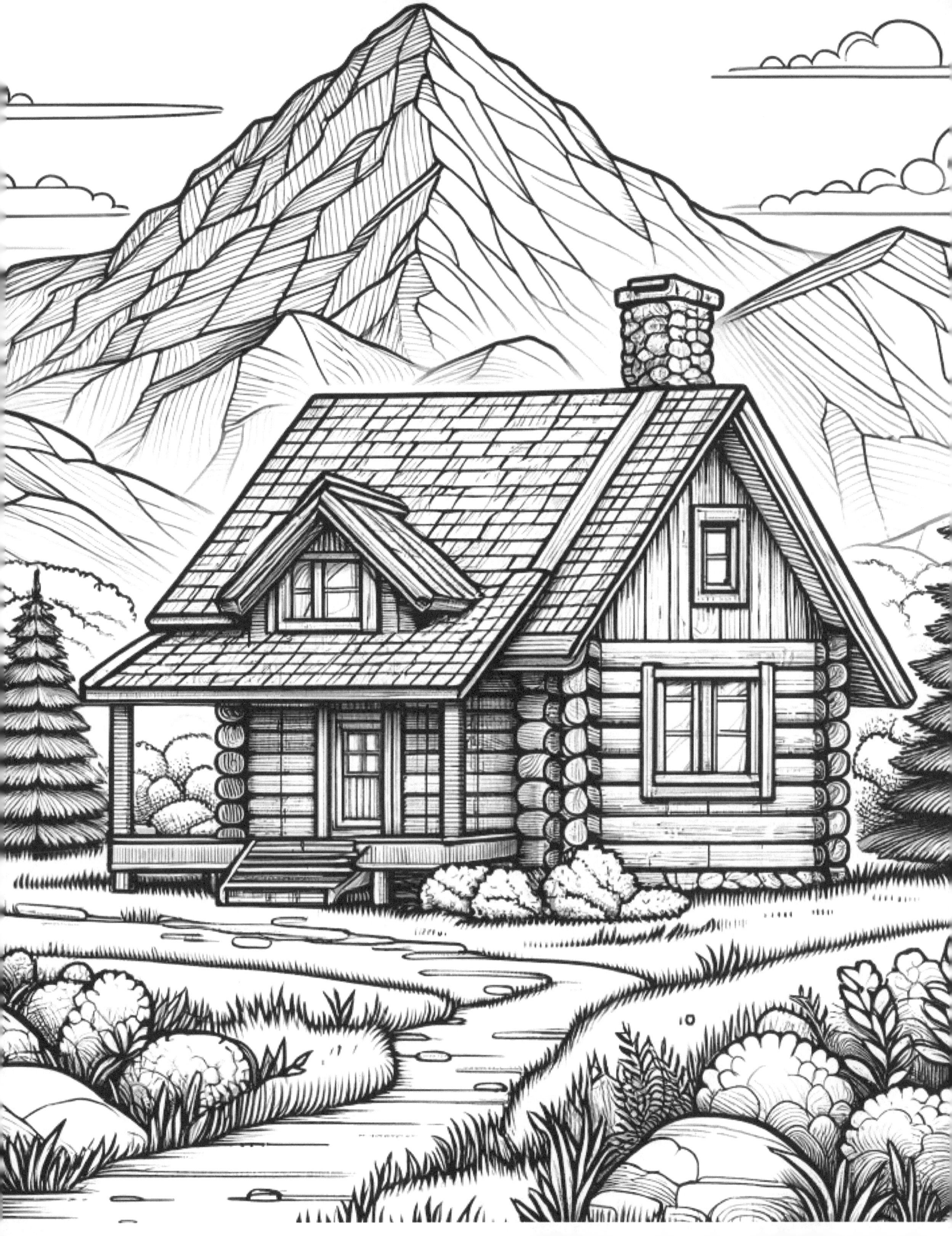

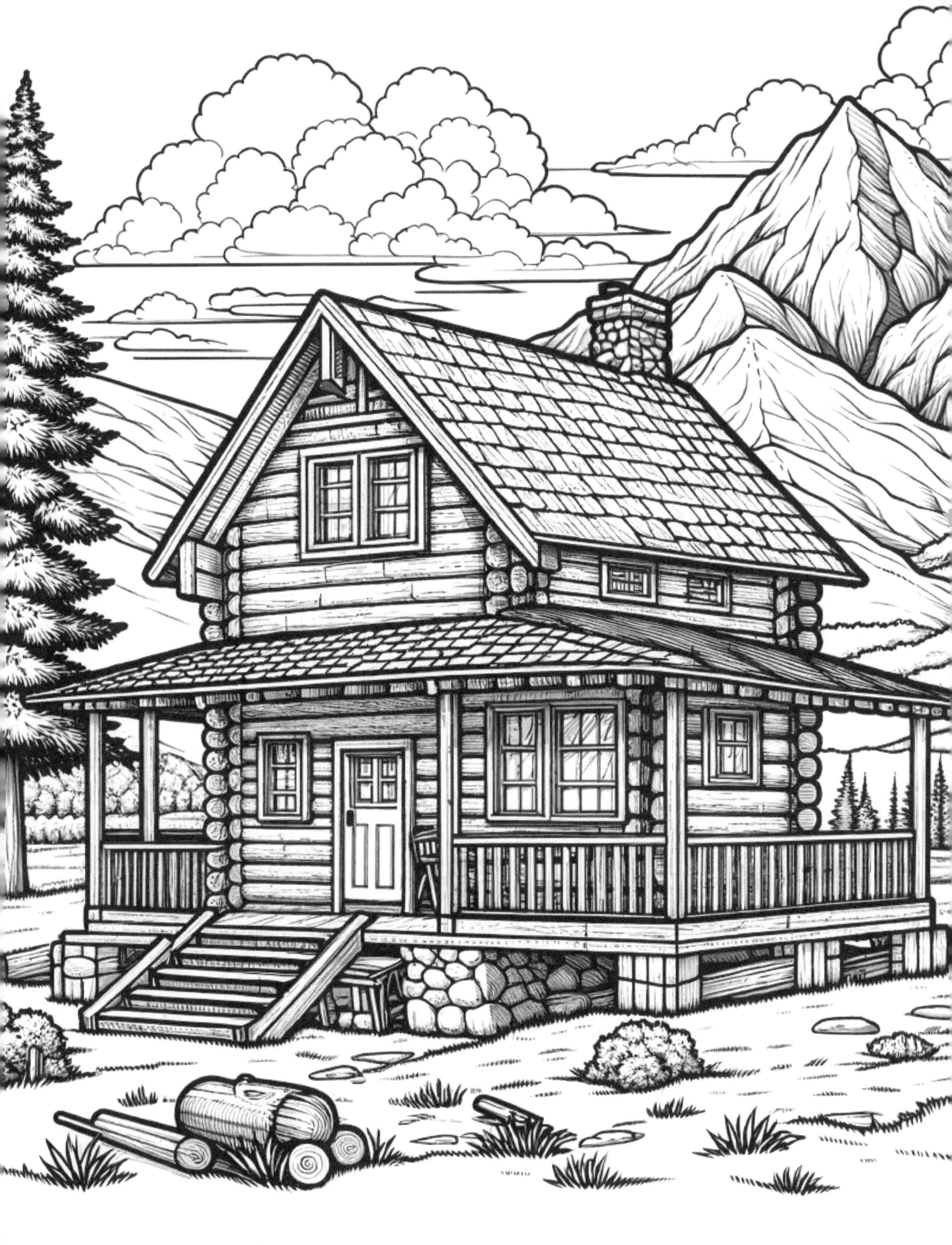

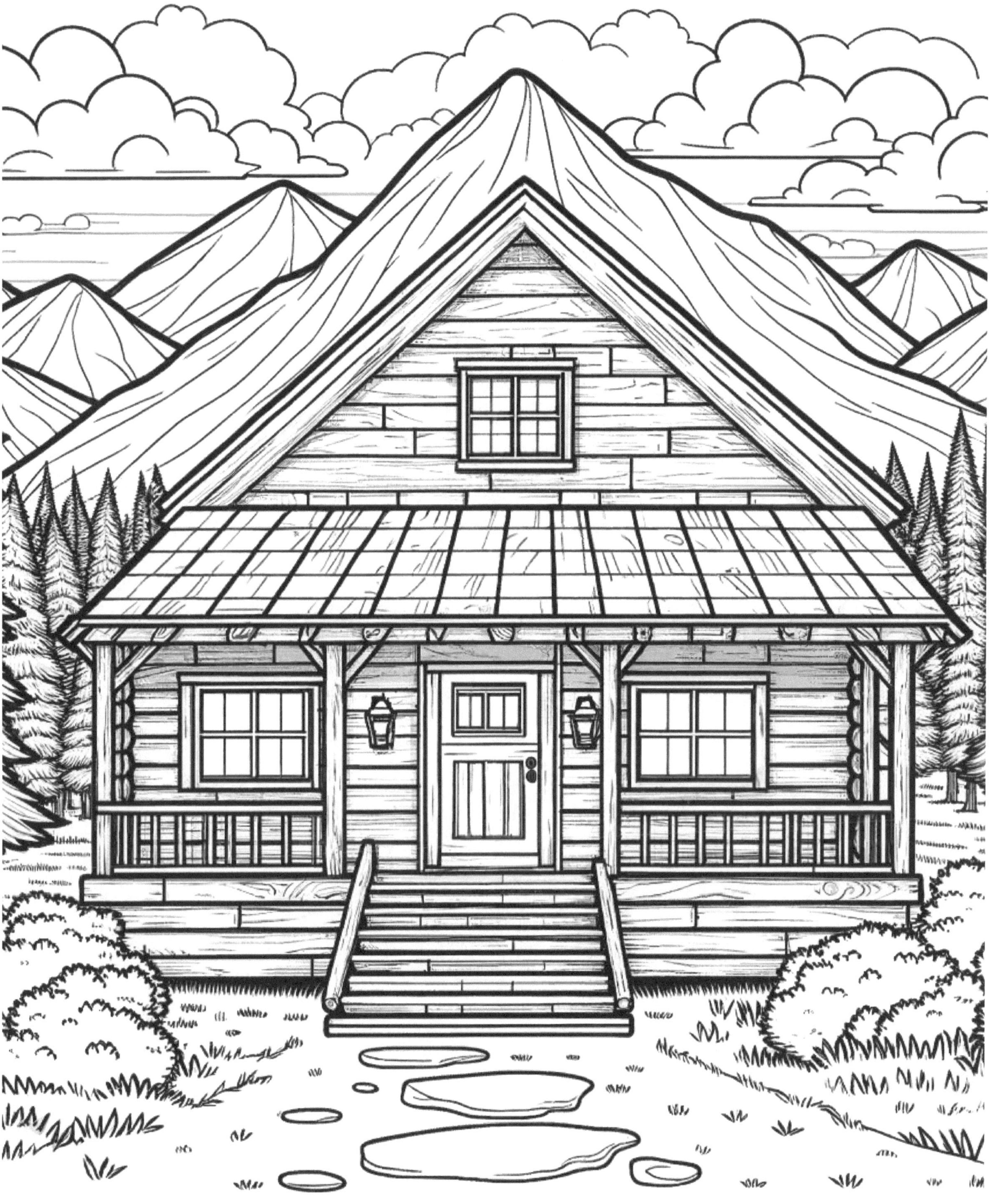

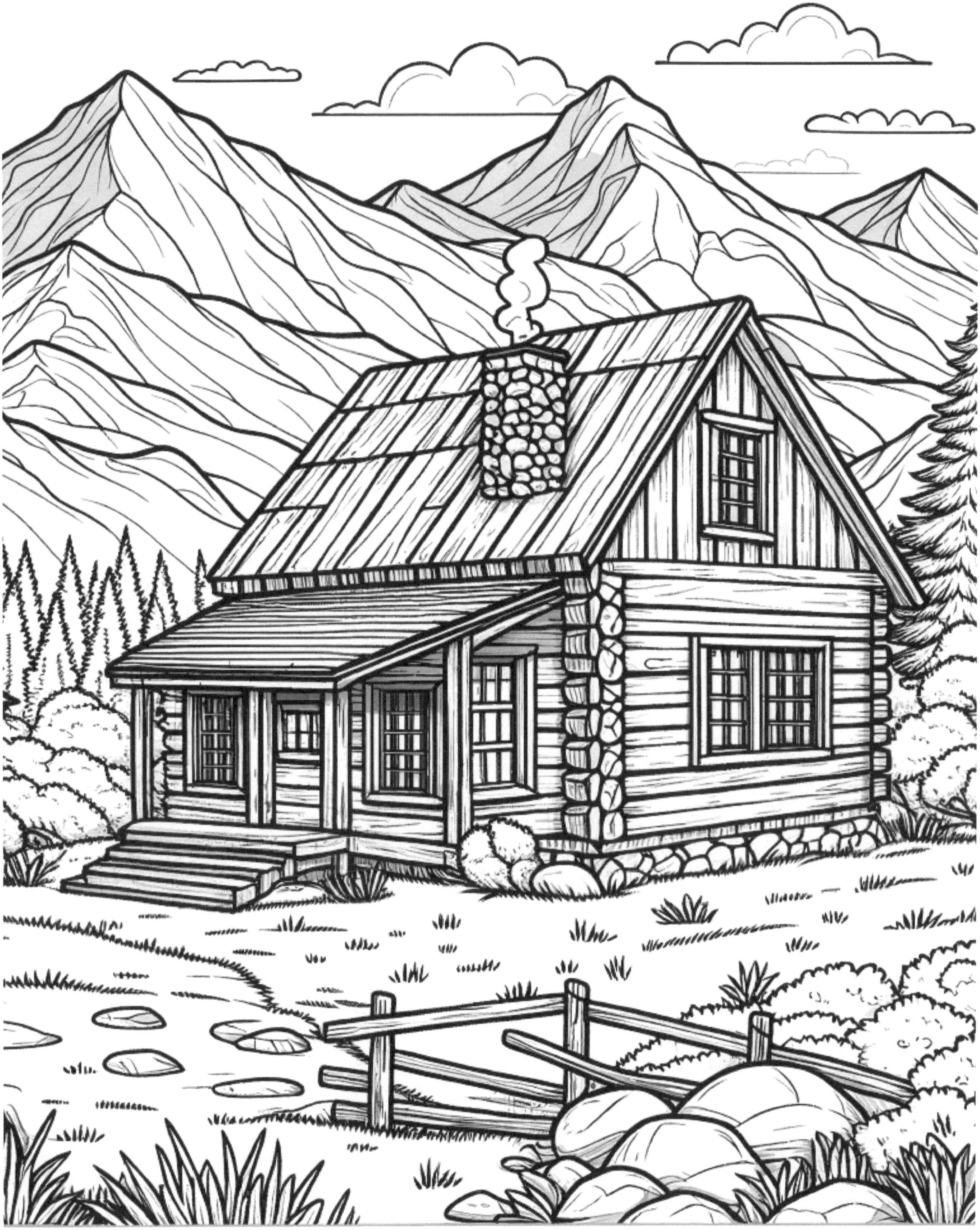

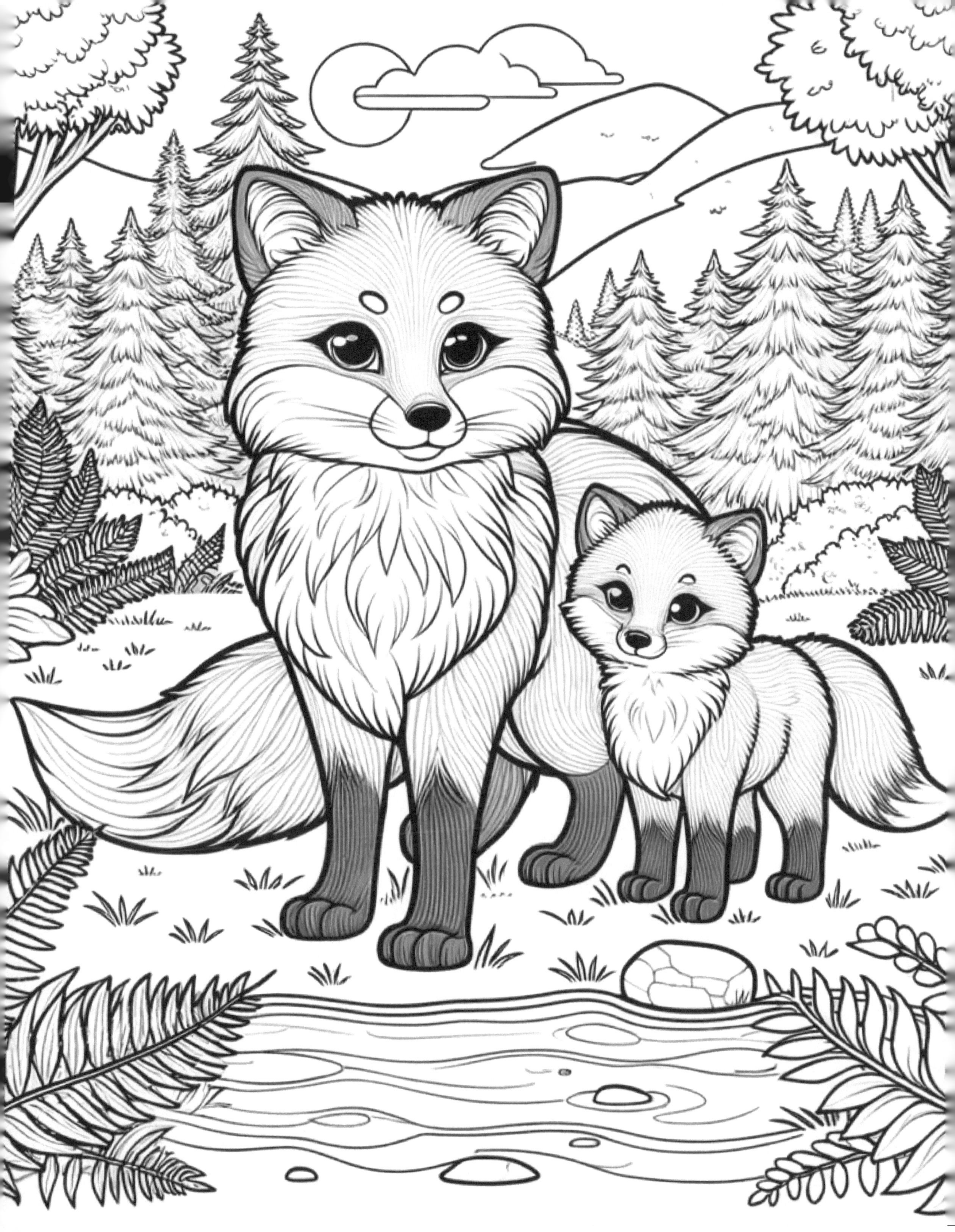

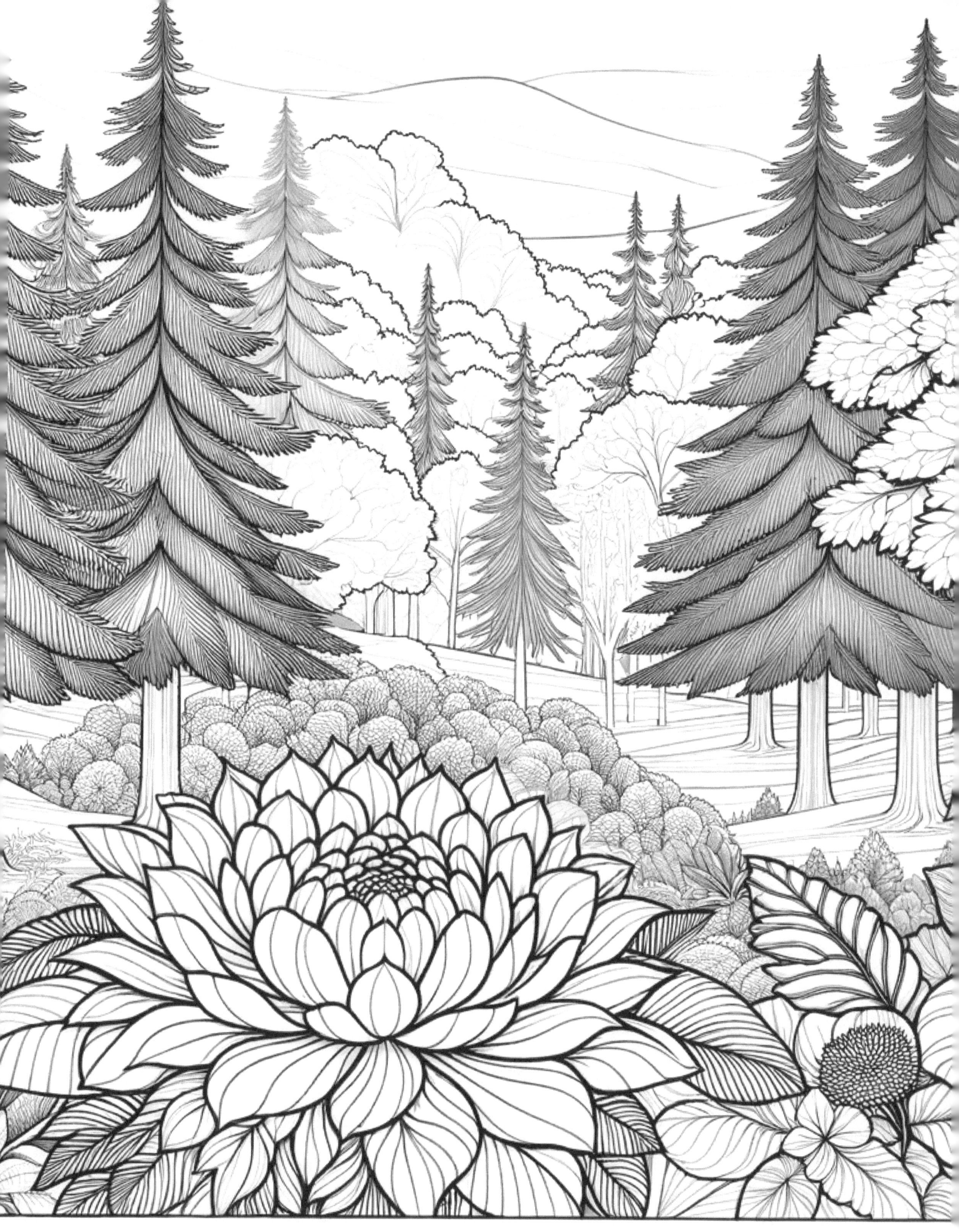

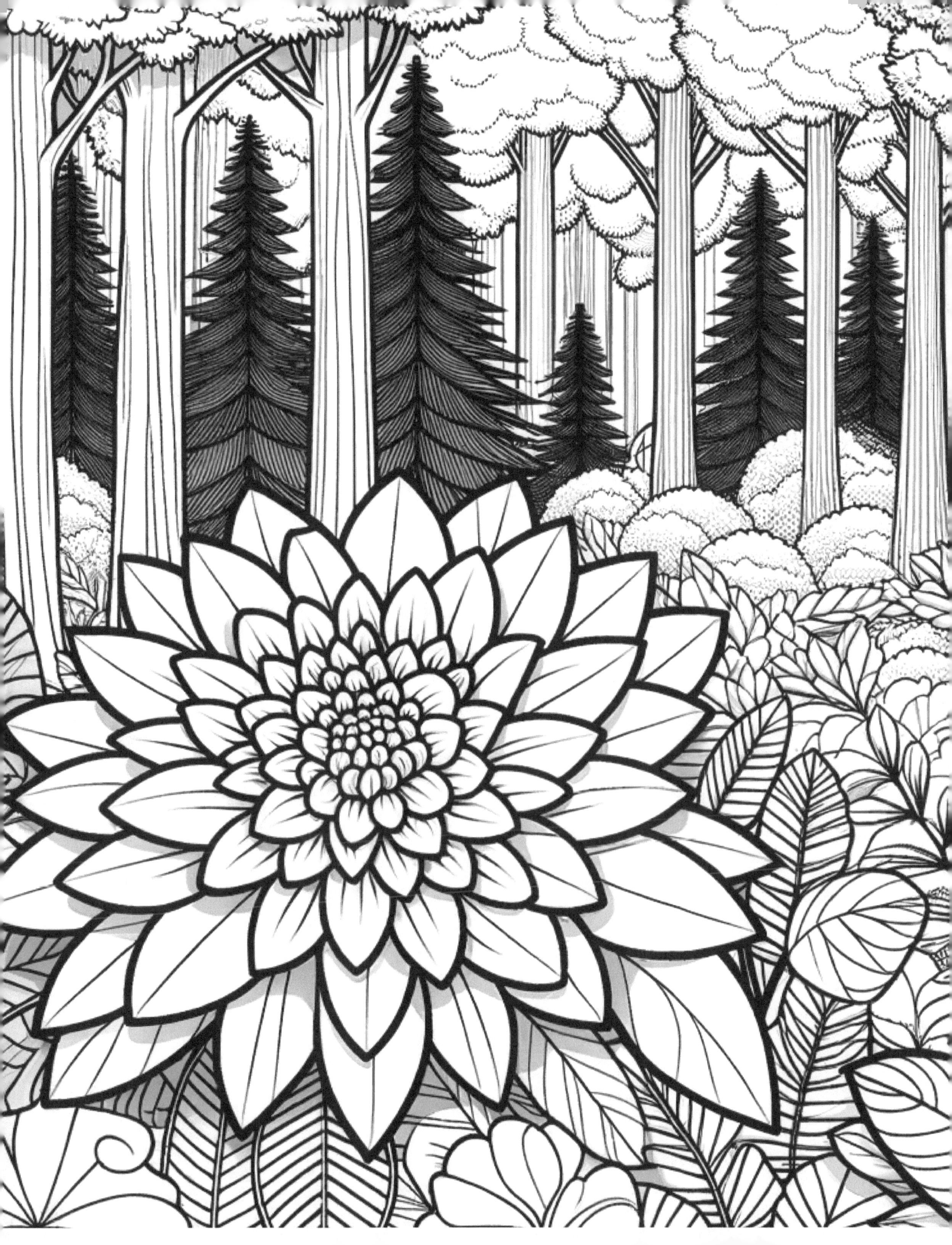

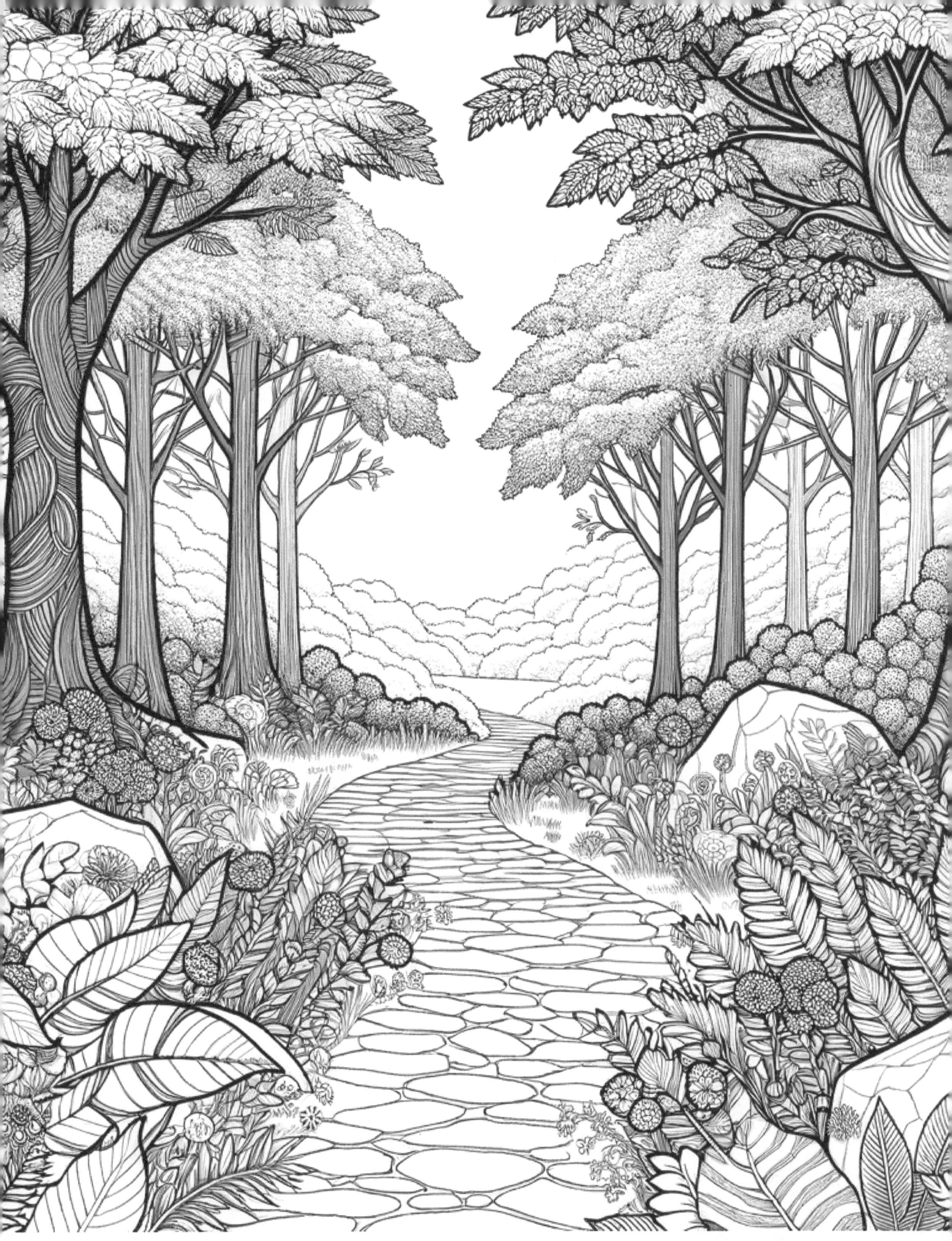

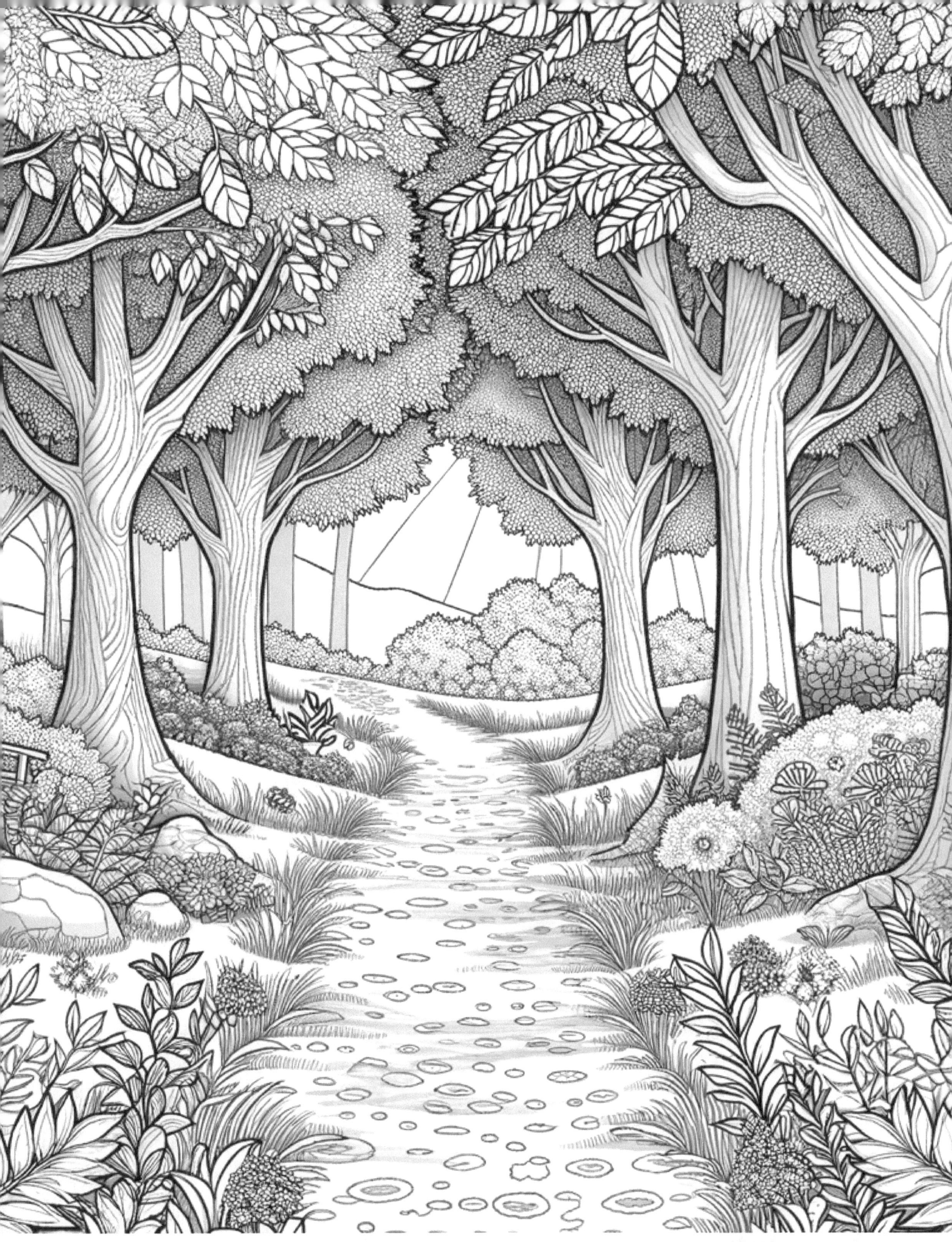

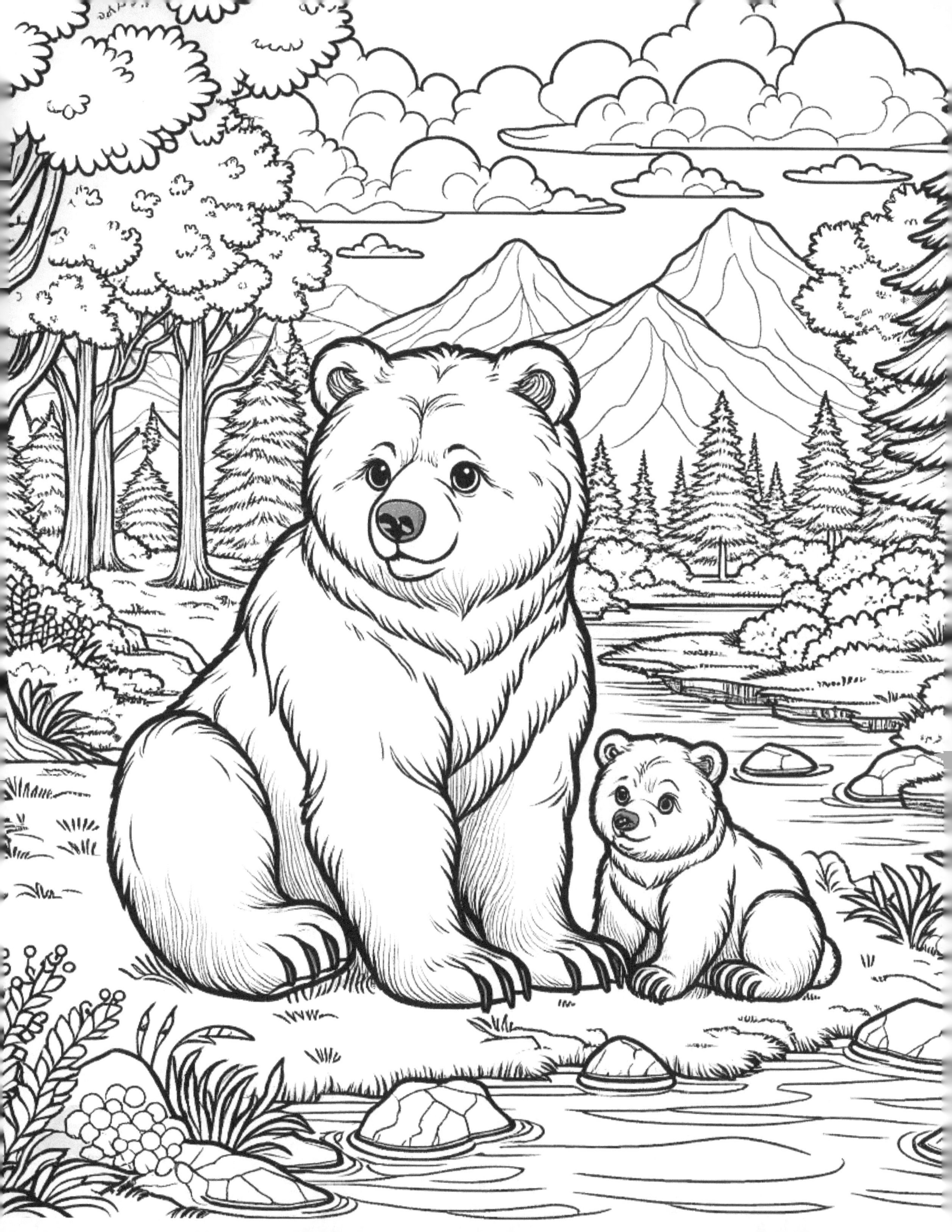

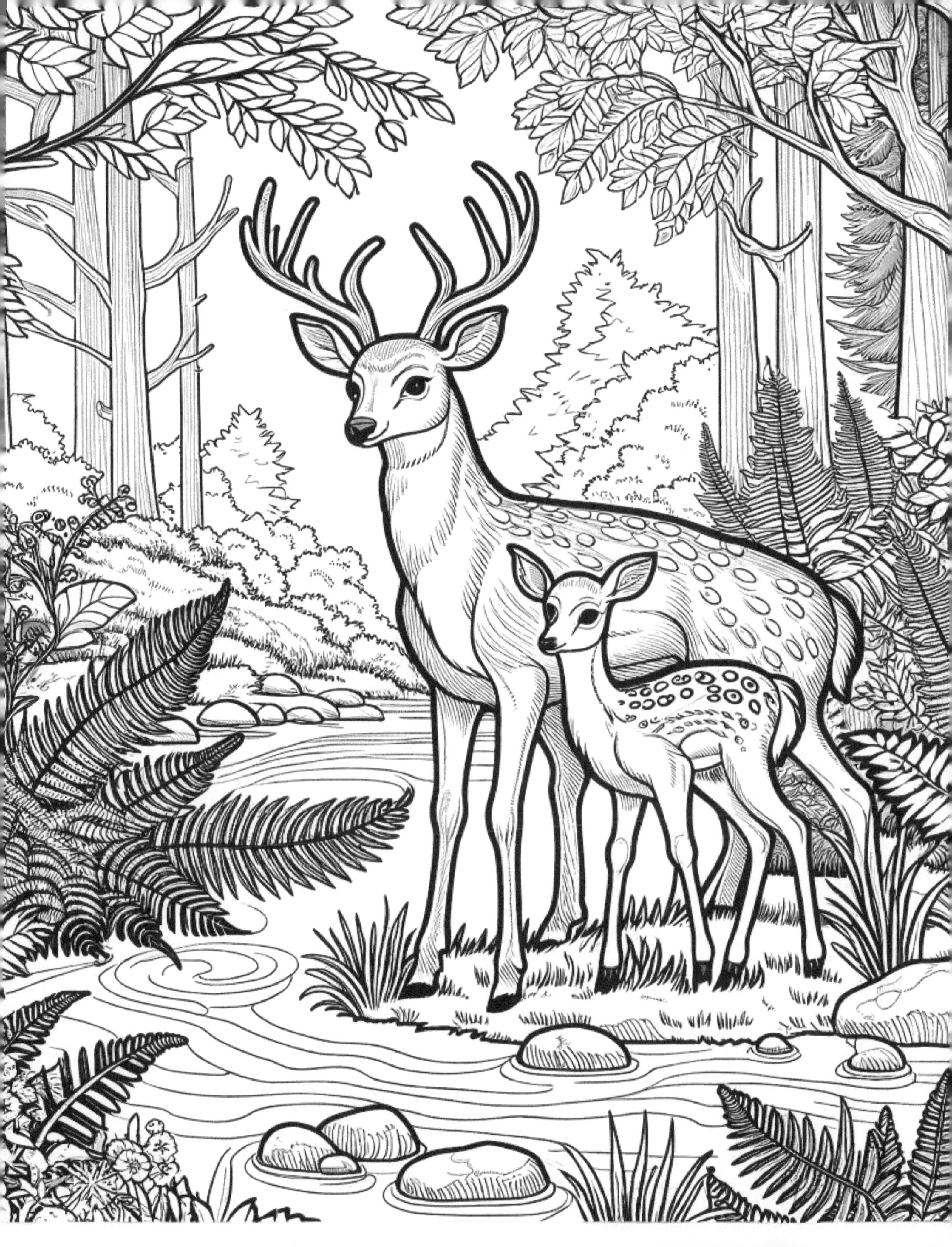

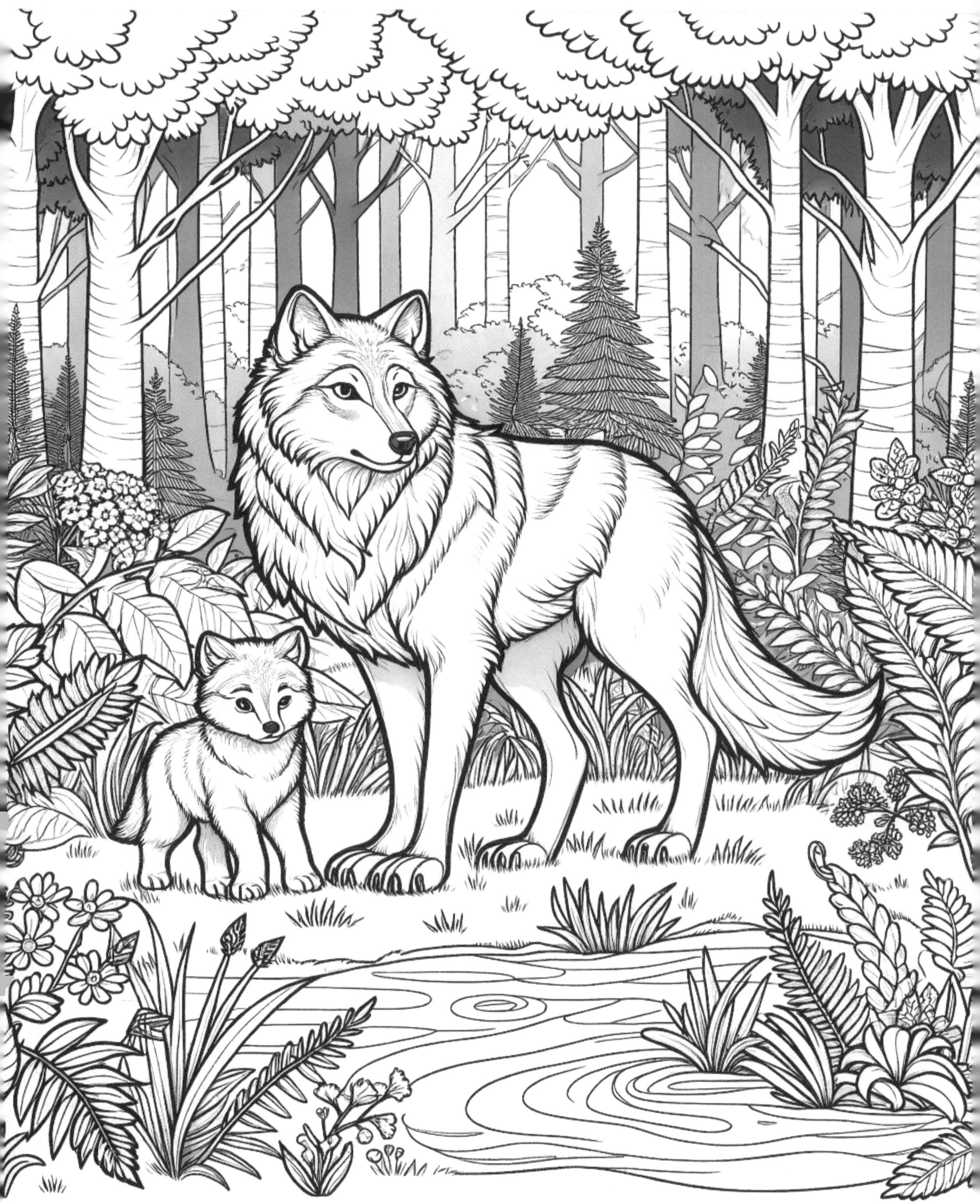

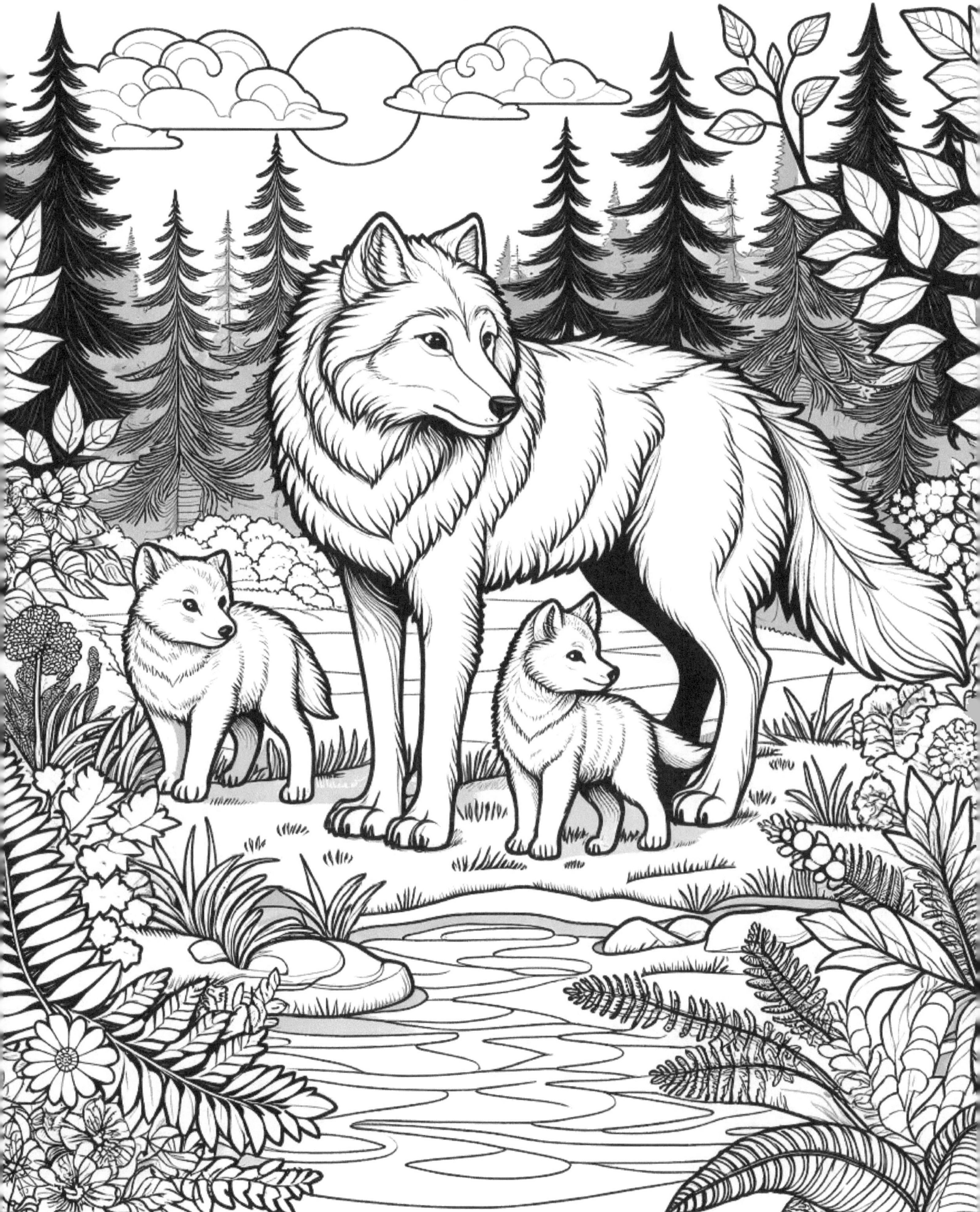

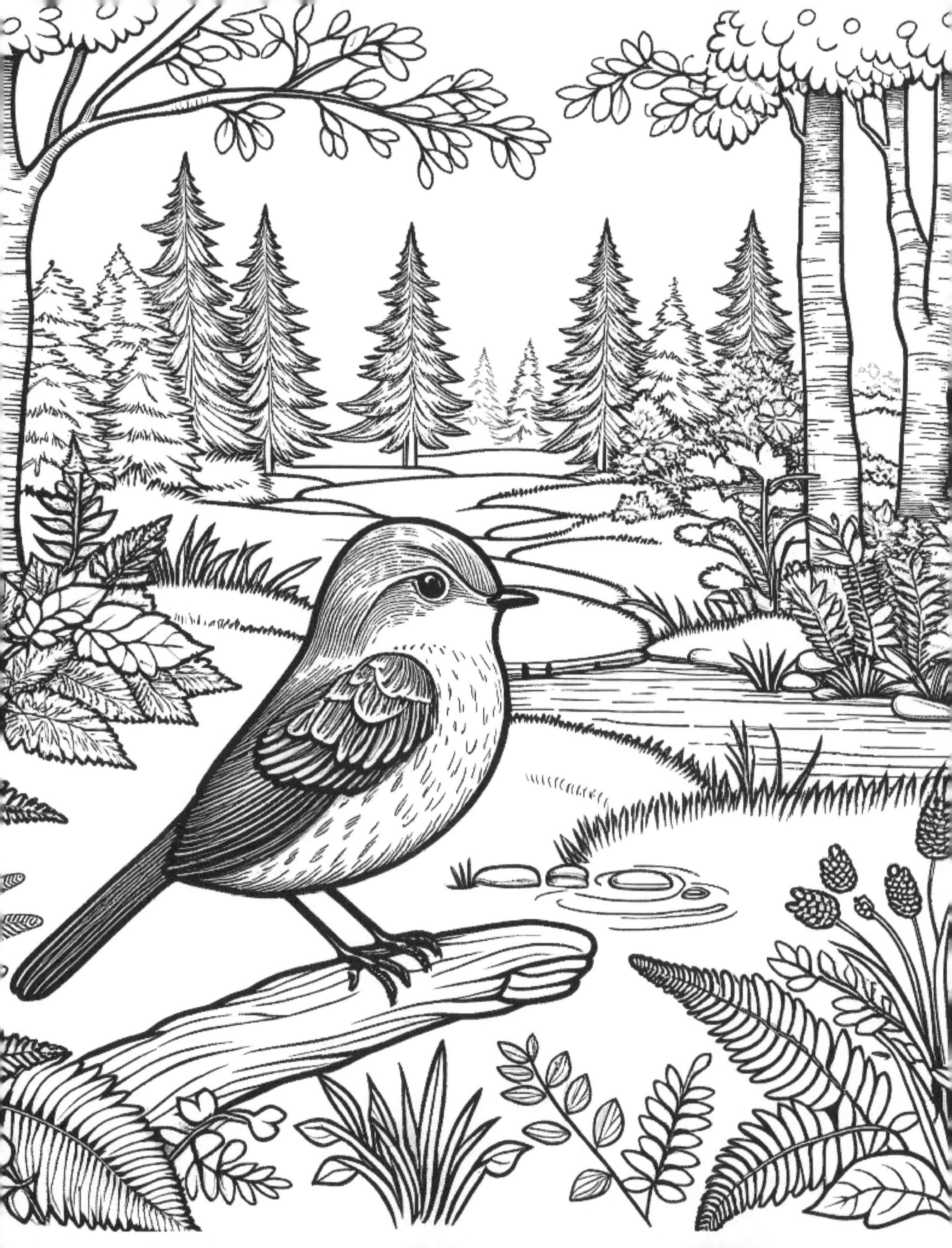

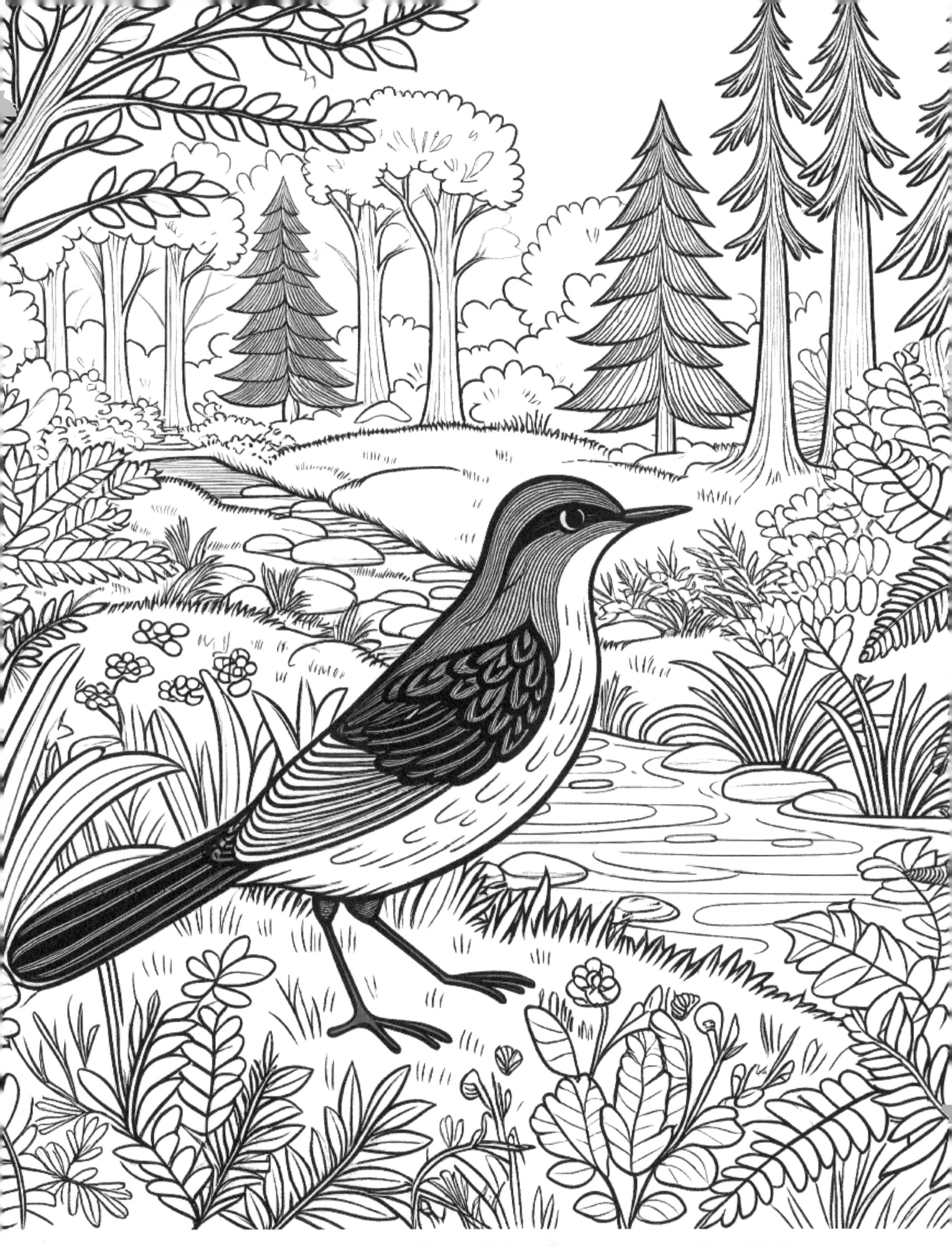

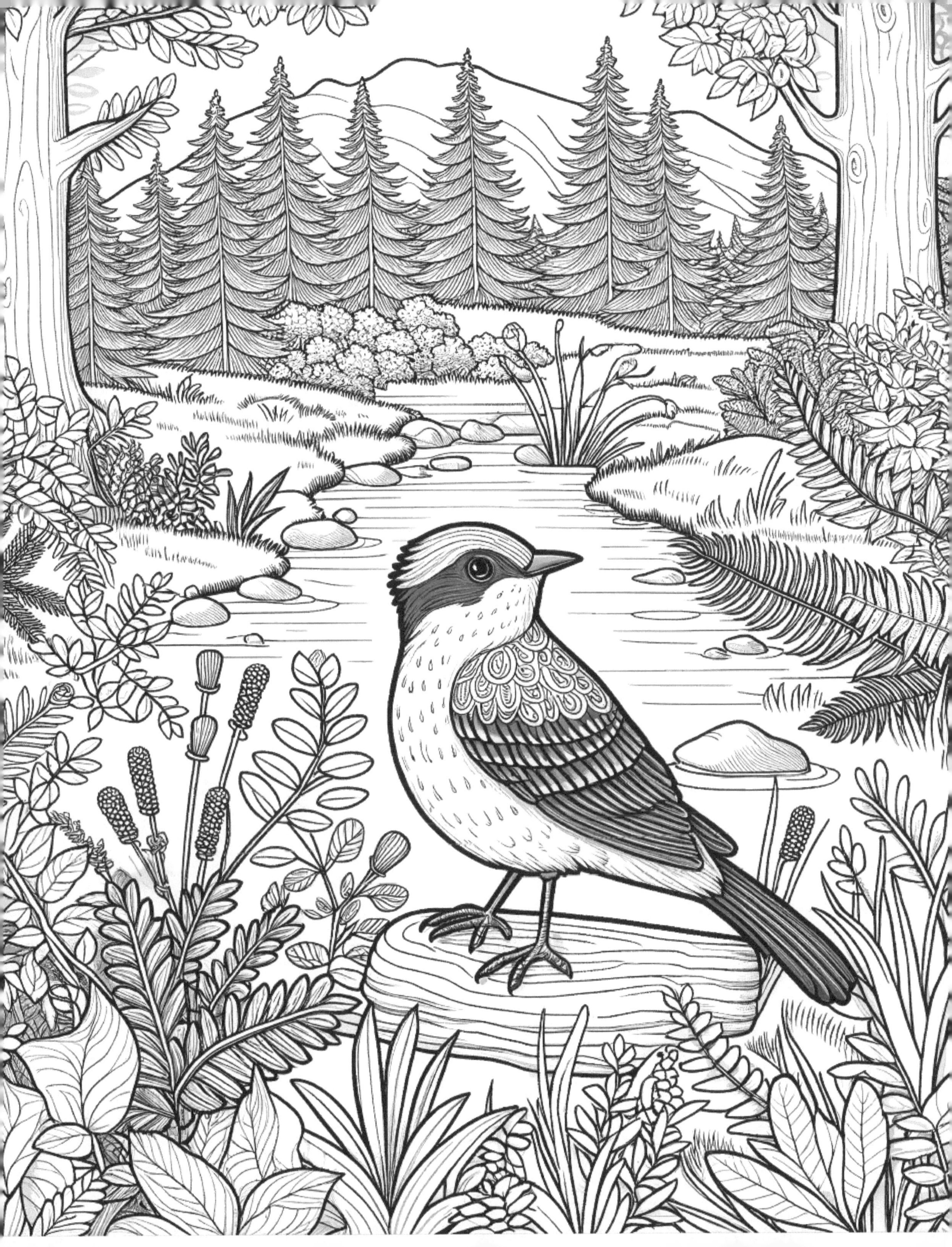

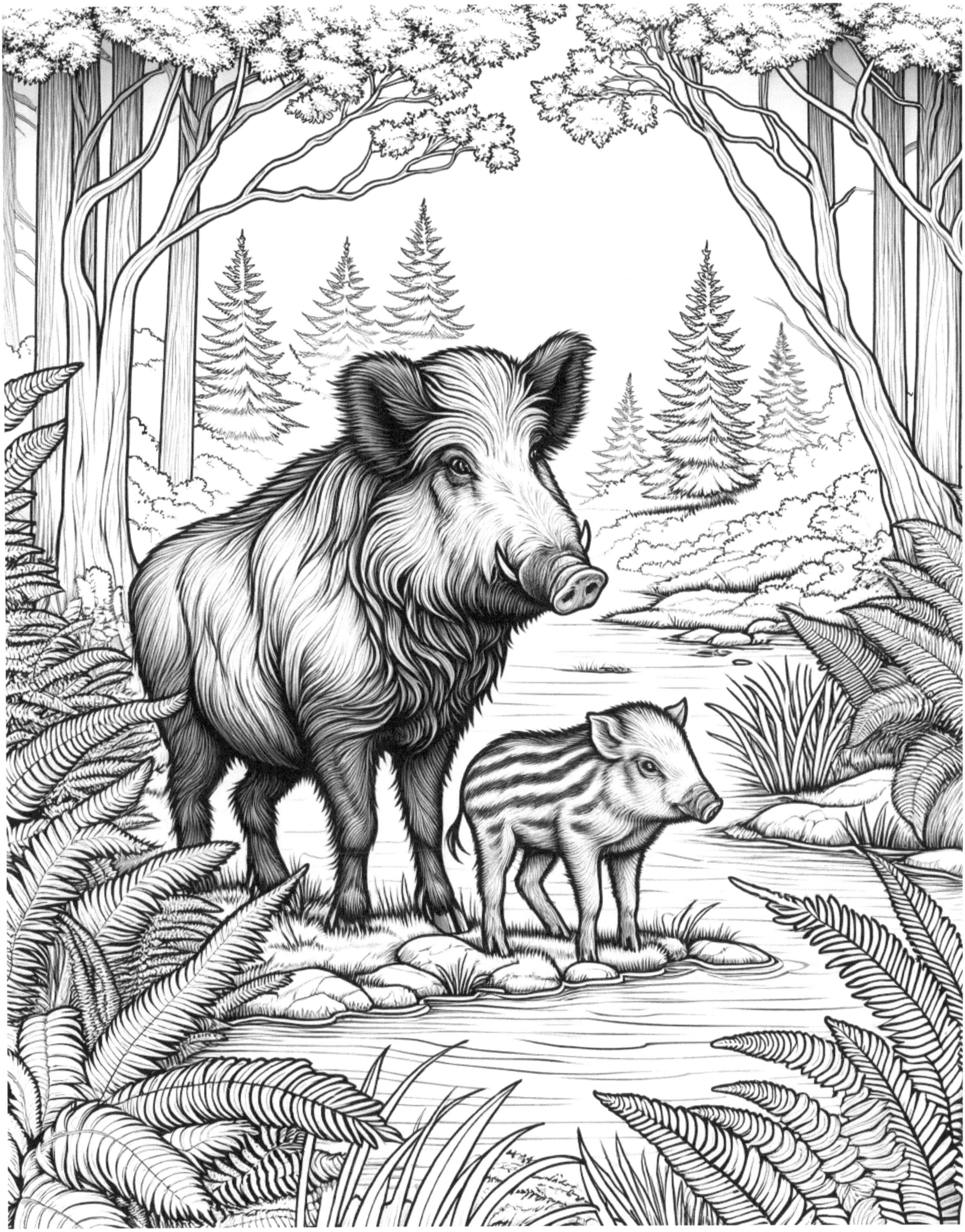

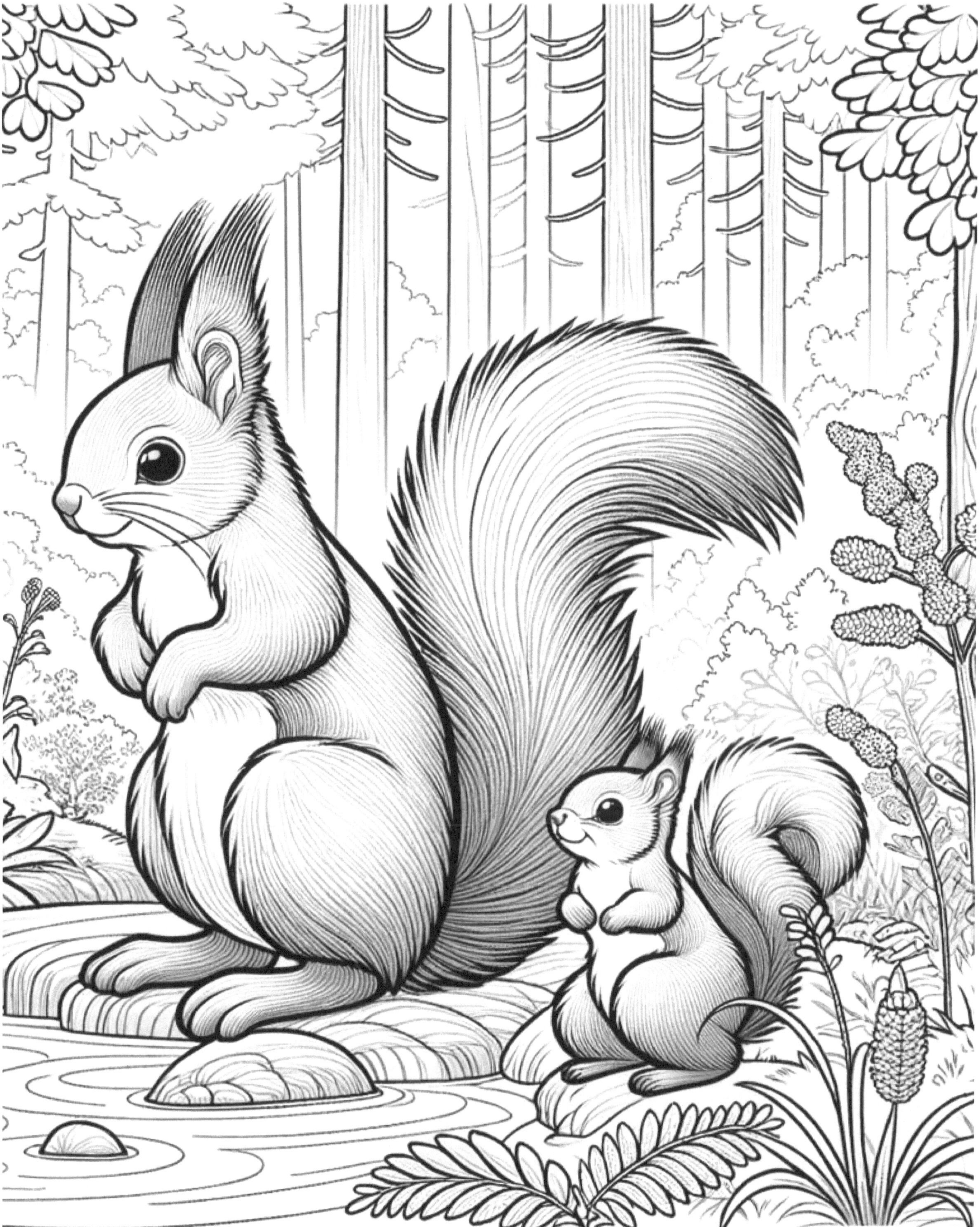

Made in United States
Troutdale, OR
05/28/2025

31714443R00038